Richard Scarry's BUSIEST

EAT AT JOE'S

CHIEF

PEOPLE EVER

Random House 🏠 New York

The busy people are on their way to work.
Bre-e-e-e-t! Sergeant Murphy blows his whistle to stop
the traffic and let the workers cross the street.

Bre-e-e-e-t! Lowly Worm and Huckle Cat are helping Sergeant Murphy direct traffic. Lowly and Huckle want to be policemen when they grow up.

Miney and Moe, the television camera bugs, take pictures of things that happen in Busytown. The pictures will be part of a television newscast.

7

clergyman

TELEVISIONS BOOKS

bookseller

optician

SPORTS EYEGLASSES

SPORT SHOP

Sergeant Murphy rides around town to make sure that everything is peaceful. If the chief of police hears of any trouble, he tells Sergeant Murphy about it over the radio.

"Sergeant Murphy! Sergeant Murphy!"
The police station is calling Murphy on the radio.
"Grocer Cat has just telephoned. His grocery store has been robbed!"

"Quickly! We must try to catch the thief!" says Sergeant Murphy.

road painter

ditch digger

SHOEMAKER

Get off that fresh cement, Mr. Frumble!

FRESH CEMENT

8

radio operator

POLICE STATION

chief of police

DELICATESSEN

CANDY

DRUGSTORE

HARDWARE

HATS

FLOWERS

druggist

ICE CREAM

EAT HATS

ice cream man

sandwich-board man

ELECTRIC SUPPLIES

GROCERIES

BANANAS

APPLES

ORANGES

flower seller

TV

Grocer Cat

Sergeant Murphy speeds through the street
on his motorcycle.
"Faster, faster!" says Lowly.
"We must catch the thief."

mailman

10

LAWYER

DANCING SCHOOL

SINGING LESSONS

WINDOW WASHING

UMBRELLAS

ICE CREAM

4

ANTIQUES

TAILOR

fireman

TV

sanitation worker

11

Stop thief!

miner

rug salesman

violinist

TV repairman

bugdozer driver

locksmith

drummer

construction worker

football player

golfer

brush salesman

magician

florist

"Look!" says Sergeant Murphy. The thief must be in that crowd of people. All of them are carrying things. How can we tell which one stole something from Grocer Cat's store?

Lowly looks at the crowd and suddenly shouts, "There's the thief!"

Lowly chases after the thief and tackles him around the legs. Who can it be?

sign paster

12

juggler

architect

lifeguard

street cleaner

lawyer

sailor

banana eater

bass fiddler

plumber

soldier

carpenter

tennis player

window washer

another tennis player

It's Bananas Gorilla! And Lowly has caught him.
"But how did you know Bananas was the thief?"
asks Sergeant Murphy.
"Well," says Lowly, "out of all those people
Bananas was the only one carrying something that
could be stolen from a grocery store."
Very good thinking, Policeman Lowly.
Take Bananas off to jail now.

13

A Visit to the Big City

Mother Cat is taking Huckle and Lowly to the city.
What do you think they are going to do there?
They have to take the train. Mother Cat
sits in the passenger coach. Huckle and Lowly
sit with the engineer in the locomotive.
To-o-o-o-t! Lowly pulls the whistle.
Off they go.

bulb changer

taxi driver

traveling
salesman

skier

scout leader

porter

mountain
climber

scouts

cook

waiter

switchman

DINING
CAR

passengers

Mother Cat

COACH

wheel inspector

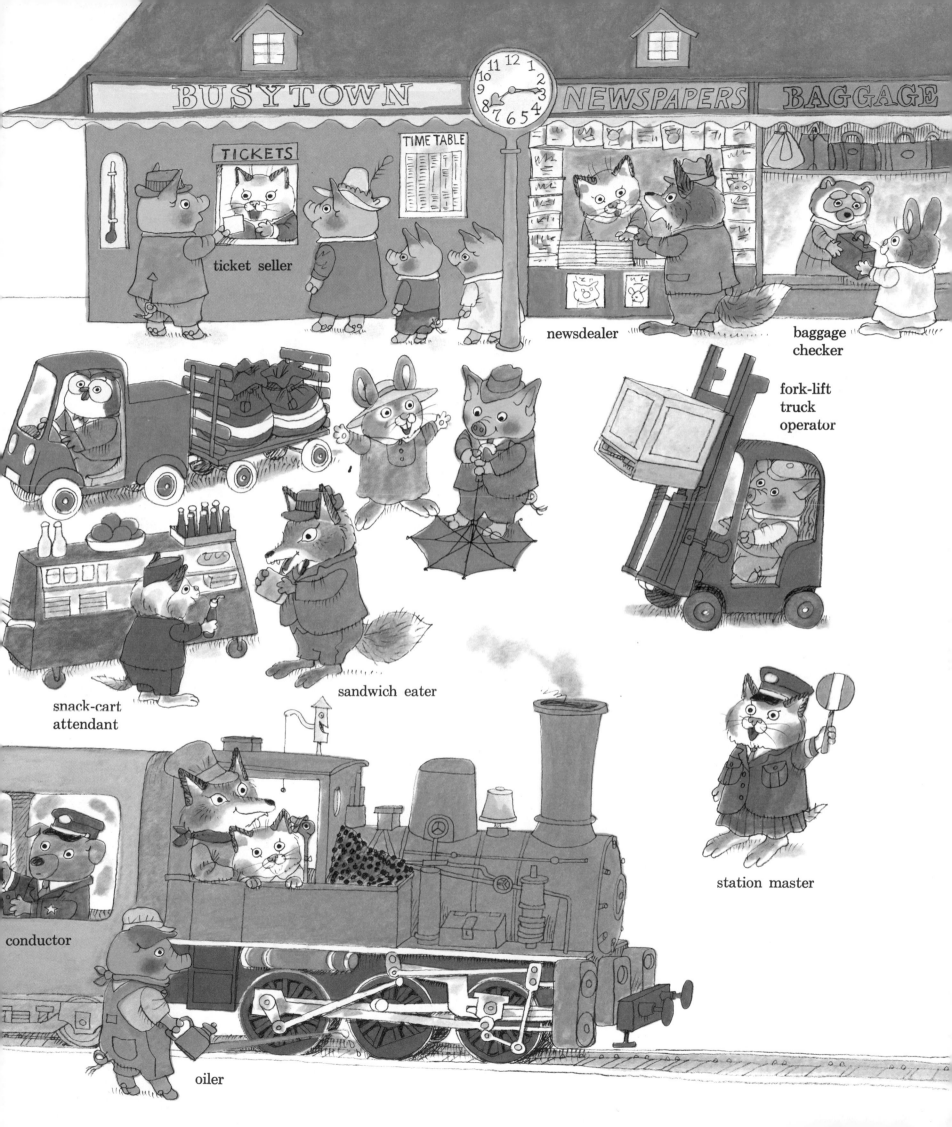

BUSYTOWN   NEWSPAPERS   BAGGAGE

TICKETS

TIME TABLE

ticket seller

newsdealer

baggage
checker

fork-lift
truck
operator

snack-cart
attendant

sandwich eater

conductor

oiler

station master

truck driver

mason

hole digger

bulldozer operator

plumber

carpenters

plumber

mason

HOUSES FOR SALE

mortar mixer

bathtub deliverymen

engineer

newspaper reader

carpenters

roofer

electrician

painter

paperhanger

gardener

SOLD

nail spiller

stove and refrigerator deliveryman

TV

The train chugs along the tracks
on the way to the big city.
Suddenly Lowly shouts, "STOP!
Something is wrong!"
The train stops.
Lowly jumps down from the locomotive
and runs to the switch.
What can the matter be?

17

engineer

school-bus driver

log cutter

log hauler

tree chopper

kite flier

18

hobo

grass mower

A freight train is speeding toward them
on the same track.
   Lowly turns the switch . . . just in time!
The freight train rolls onto another track.
Lowly has saved everyone from a terrible accident.
Lowly is certainly a good railroad worker, isn't he?

*Watch out,
Mr. Frumble!*

ICE
CREAM

19

TRAVEL   GIFT SHOP   BAGGAGE ROOM   FLOWERS

FLY

COME TO LAND

MAIL

TRACK 3

mail-cart driver

TRACK 2

sleeper

workers running
to catch their train

sweeper

TRACK 1

SNACK BAR NEWSSTAND

window washer

clock fixer

EXIT

jewelry seller

TICKETS

TIMETABLE

TO TAXIS

porter

pencil seller

Finally the train arrives
at the city railroad station.
What a big, busy place it is!
Look! Someone is there to greet
the three arrivals. Who can he be?

21

steel
workers

sidewalk superintendent

welder

crane operator

foreman

cement mixer

NOW BUILDING
A NEW
SKYSCRAPER

TV1

The owner of the television station
has come to meet them. A few days ago
he invited Huckle and Lowly to appear
on a television show.

He drives them through the city streets
to the television station.

22

CONTROL BOOTH

musicians

cameraman

TV 1

TV1

TAXI

doorman

In the television studio,
Huckle and Lowly sing a jolly song.
People all over the country can see
and hear the program on their
television sets.

When Huck and Lowly return to Busytown,
all their friends will tell them that they
saw the program, too.

Grandma Cat lives far away, but she sees
Huckle and Lowly on her television set.
She is very surprised and pleased.
"I must visit my two television entertainers
soon," she says.
Would YOU like to be a television singer, too?

Mr. Frumble's Bad Day

Mr. Frumble is going to work.
He forgot to open the garage doors
before he backed the car out.
What a bad way to start the day!

butcher

TV

check-out person

There are a few things
Mr. Frumble must do on his way
to work. First, he stops to shop
at the supermarket. Look at
what he's done now!

manager

book borrowers

librarian

Next, he goes to the library to borrow a book.
The librarian does not like noisy sneezers.

barber

druggist

At the barber shop he fidgets so much that
the barber cuts his necktie by mistake.

Mr. Frumble has a little accident when he
buys some vitamin pills from the druggist.

Then he tries on a suit at the clothing store.
"I think you need a larger size, Mr. Frumble."

He tries on a hat.
"Don't pull it down so hard, Mr. Frumble."

laundress

He washes his laundry at the laundromat.
"I think you put too much soap in the machine,
Mr. Frumble."

nurse

At Dr. Lion's office he breaks the scales.
Does Mr. Frumble weigh THAT much?

At the dentist's he looks to see what
Dr. Dentist is doing to Tillie's teeth.
"Please sit down and wait your turn,
Mr. Frumble."

waitress

chef

waiter

Mr. Frumble goes into a restaurant to eat his lunch.
He sees the chef cooking some Flaming Bananas.

Mr. Frumble thinks the fire is dangerous.
He throws water on it.

The chef is furious.
"I NEED fire to cook my Flaming Bananas,"
he says. "Now you have ruined them."

The angry chef frightens Mr. Frumble.
He runs out of the restaurant.
Oops! Watch where you are going, Mr. Frumble.

bank
teller

DRIVE-IN BANK

teacher

pupils

SCHOOL

Bananamobile driver

POST OFFICE

post-office clerk

Mr. Frumble gets back into his car, but
again he doesn't look where he is going.
He runs into a water hydrant and
accidentally puts out another fire
on the chef's Flaming Bananas.

THE DAILY EAGLE

typist

editor

newsboy

TV

photographer

reporter

MUSIC SHOP

RESTAURANT

OUR SPECIALTY—
FLAMING BANANAS

chimney
sweep

AUTOMOBILES

BIKE SHOP

THE
COFFEE
POT

COFFEE

automobile salesman

newspaper
deliveryman

NEWSPAPER
DELIVERY

linotypist

pressmen

29

bulldozer operator

bugdozer operator

road leveler

dump-truck driver

GAS

Mr. Frumble!
How did you ever get your car on that new road?
It's not ready yet for drivers. The workers are
still busy building it.
Get off immediately.
You have certainly had a bad day, haven't you,
Mr. Frumble?

pumpkin-car driver

gas-station attendant

car greaser

30

roller operator

dump-truck driver

"It's about time you went home," Lowly tells Mr. Frumble, "before you cause any more trouble. I will call a tow truck for you."

SOS

pilot

tow-truck driver

A tow truck comes and takes Mr. Frumble home.

So long, Mr. Frumble. You didn't even get to work today. Maybe things will be better tomorrow.

tugboat skipper

lightship captain

crane operator

helmsman

ship's captain

lobsterman

straddle-truck driver

fork-lift truck driver

taxi driver

Down by the Busy Sea

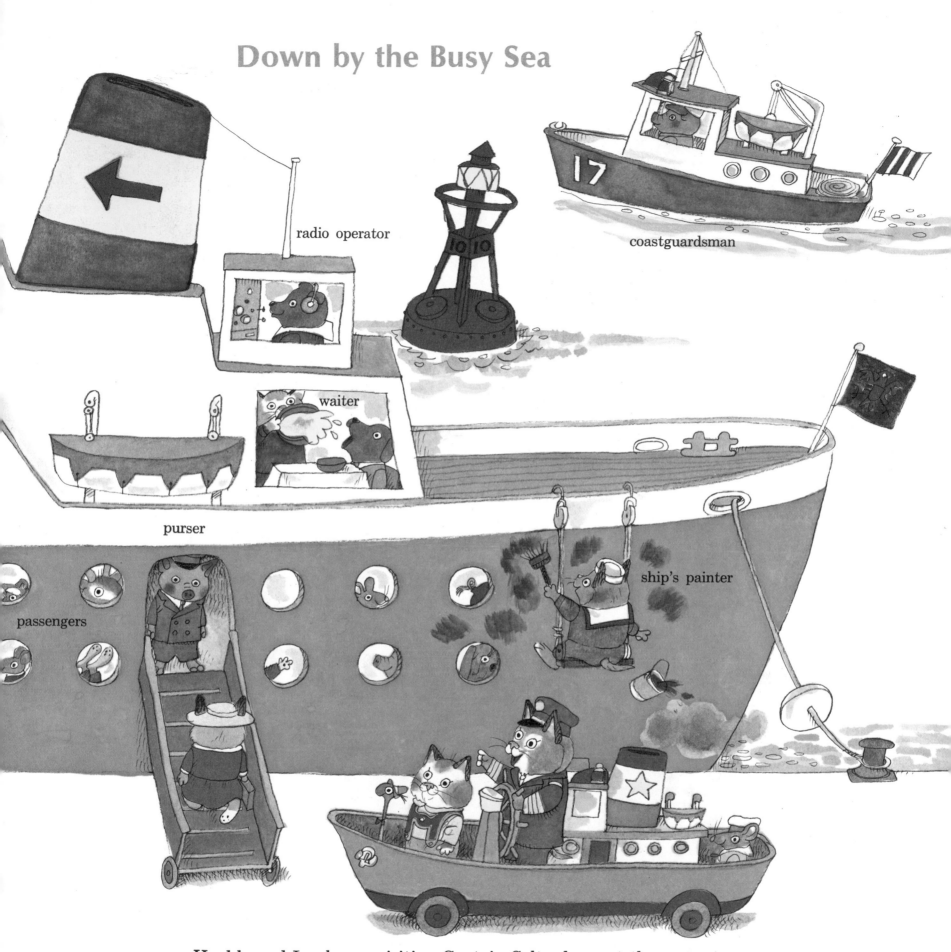

radio operator

coastguardsman

waiter

purser

passengers

ship's painter

Huckle and Lowly are visiting Captain Salty down at the seaport.
The captain shows them all the things there are to see at a harbor.
"This is a passenger ship," he explains. "It will carry people
across the ocean to visit their friends in distant places."
Lowly thinks *he* would like to be a sea captain when he grows up.

lighthouse keeper

fishermen

sailor

Next, Captain Salty points to a cargo ship.
"It can carry all kinds of things to distant ports,"
he says. "Right now cars are being loaded into its hold.
The ship will carry them across the sea, and people in
faraway countries will drive them."
"LOOK!" cries Captain Salty loudly.
"There is a fire on that barge. We must help!
Hop onto the fireboat. Let's go!"

captain

cargo
handlers

fireboat
captain

fork-lift
truck driver

harbor
police

giant-crane
operator

dockside engineer

35

submarine skipper

Mr. Frumble,
the boat wrecker

The fireboat rushes
toward the burning barge
and sprays it with water.

ferryboat captain

FERRY

36

fireboat firemen

lazy fisherman

Captain Tillie has jumped off the burning barge.
"Help! Help!" she cries.
Lowly jumps overboard with a life preserver
to save her.

A wet Captain Tillie thanks Lowly
and gives him a big kiss. Isn't it
amazing that such a little fellow
can rescue such a big sea captain?
Good work, Sea Captain Lowly.

37

hay baler

tractor driver

cabbage picker

grass mower

farm hand

woodcutter

poster man

CHEW

wall builder

hay lifter

fence builder

Grandma Cat Comes to Visit

Grandma Cat is coming to visit the Cat family.
The whole family drives to the airport to meet her.

As the car passes Farmer Goat's farm, Lowly asks,
"Can we stop and buy some apples?"

Father Cat says, "No. We don't want to be late
getting to the airport."

surveyor

windmill
fixer

apple picker

lightning rod
installer

apple gatherer

applesauce cooker

corn picker

APPLES

apple seller

apple eater

water pumper

pumpkin seller

39

glider pilot

helicopter pilot

air-traffic controller

radar controller

weatherman

ramp agent

They arrive at the airport ahead of time.
While they wait for Grandma's plane to come in,
Lowly visits the pilot's cockpit in a plane
that will soon take off. Now he would like to be
an airplane pilot instead of a sea captain.
Huckle visits the airport control tower.
He would like to be an air-traffic controller
and tell the planes when to land and take off.
What would YOU like to do at an airport?

pilot

copilot

flight engineer

flight attendant

pilot

WAITING ROOM

BUSYTOWN AIRPORT

TO ALL FLIGHTS

CHECK-IN COUNTER

TAXI

Mr. Frumble, the
upside-down pilot

parachutist

balloonist

FOLLOW
ME

airplane washer

flight attendant

SWISSAIR

fuel man

mailman

baggage handler

FUEL

AIRMAIL
POST OFFICE

AIR CARGO

GRANDMA'S
APPLE PIES

Here comes Grandma's plane now.
But why is she traveling on a big cargo plane?
Why isn't she on a passenger plane?

*Mr. Frumble!
You're washing
the wrong plane!*

food-delivery
person

Well! It seems that Grandma was bringing
so many apples with her that she had to come
on a cargo plane. Grandma plans to make lots
of apple pies during her visit.
   "Hi, Grandma. It's good to see you,"
says Huckle.
   "And all your apples, too," says Lowly.

Busy House Workers

Grandma is happy to be
visiting so many busy workers.

Lowly works hard
to make his bed.

Huckle works to make
his room neat.

Little Sister empties
a wastebasket.

Daddy washes the dirty dishes.

Mommy cooks the meals for the family.

And Grandma and Lowly
work hard making lots
of apple pies to eat.
Lowly is especially
good at peeling apples.

44

While the apple pies are baking in the oven,
they all watch the television news of the week.

They see Lowly,
the policeman, capturing
Bananas Gorilla.

They see Lowly,
the railroad worker,
saving the train.

They see Huckle and Lowly
singing on television.

They see Lowly,
the sea captain,
saving Captain Tillie.

After seeing all those jobs, Lowly, what would you
like best of all to be when you grow up?
"Why," says Lowly, "I think best of all I would
like to be an apple-pie eater."
Well, Lowly, I think that is very nice work indeed.

Would YOU like to help Lowly eat apple pies?